Pick Me, Pick Me!

Story by: Elijah and Isaiah Smith with LaDonna Smith.
Illustrated by: Kenny Badana

ISBN: 978-0692922309 [Follow Your Dreams Publishing)

ISBN-10: 069292230X

Library of Congress Control Number: 2017914347
Follow Your Dreams Publishing, Albany, NY

Copyright 2017 by LaDonna N. Smith. All rights reserved. no part of this publication may be reproduced, stored in a retrieval system, *or* transmitted in any form *or* by any means, electronic, mechanical, photocopying, recording, *or* otherwise without permission of the author. For *more* information regarding permission, e-mail: info@Fydpublishing.com
www.Fydpublishing.com

This book is dedicated to all of the little ballers with big game!

Here is a little boy who loves basketball, and his name is Cree.
He's a great basketball player, but compared to some of his friends sometimes he felt like he was only two foot three.

However, he has the passion and drive to be great.
He practiced every day until his mom yelled, "Cree, it's getting kind of late!"

One day, Cree asked his mother why he was so short,
and why everyone picked the tall kids first to play on the basketball court.
"Baby, some people will always judge a book by its cover."
She continued, "But Cree take it from your mother.
It's not the cover that's important.
It's what's on the pages.
And if they ever opened your book, they would see you are simply amazing."

The next morning, Cree woke his dad up early to practice his game. He even wanted to keep practicing when it began to rain.

He put some salt in his shoes and some pep in his step,
but the school bus was coming, so to the corner, he leapt.

In gym class, when it was time to pick teams,
no one ever wanted to pick Wayne or Cree.
Wayne was just too clumsy, and Cree was way too short. They could never score a basket, is what the other players thought.

"You're much too short Cree," the star player, Keith, laughed. "You're even shorter than some of the girls in our class."

On game day, Cree raised his hand high for Coach Dave to see, but Coach Dave ignored him and decided to play Keith.

"Pick me, Coach Dave, I am good, and I am quick.
I can dribble the ball, and I can even assist. I can post up, I can get the ball in the hoop,.
I can play defense, and I can really shoot."

"That's nice, Cree," said Coach Dave.
"But I can't promise to put you in the game.
Now sit on the bench, and watch, and learn.
Maybe when you're bigger, you'll get a turn."

Cree couldn't stand it when Coach Dave got in his way.
He wanted to do what he loved; he just wanted to play.

Cree warmed the bench during games, and he cheered for his team, but he got so bored that he started to daydream.

Cree dreamt he was playing basketball in outer space. Down the paint, through the hoop, a smile on coach's face.

Suddenly Coach Dave sprung to his feet, and the crowd grew quiet because something serious happened to Keith.

Coach Dave called the team into a huddle.

"We are three points down, and our team is in trouble.

Keith is hurt, but we won't retreat."

"Pick me, pick me!" yelled a persistent Cree.

Coach Dave didn't look happy; he didn't think Cree could help the team win the game.
He would rather leave Keith in the game or even put in clumsy Wayne. Coach Dave shouted, "OK Cree. I'll put you in the game." But before Cree could celebrate, coach called some players out by name.
"Pass the ball to Carl, then pass it to Reese. You can pass it to Shane, but don't pass it to Cree."

Cree was angry and wanted to just quit,
but he remembered his mom always said, "Get back up when the game gives you a hit."

Cree moved across the court with grace and ease, he set a screen for Reese
and he stole the ball from the star player on the other team.

No one could catch Cree. He was just too quick
because all of his practice had done the trick.

Cree was so excited to finally have the ball.

He made a three-pointer, and the crowd began to roar.

Dribble, dribble, dribble, dribble. Cree passed the ball down the middle.

However he didn't pass the ball to Carl, and he didn't pass it to Reese. He passed it to the other player his team thought deserved the ball the least.

Cree made his way down the court, and he dribbled pass Shane.

He did a crossover and passed the ball to Wayne.

Hurry, hurry, stop, and pop.
Cree hoped Wayne could beat the clock.
Five...Four...Three...Two...One!

Swish!

Wayne beat the buzzer

and the Bulldogs won!

A

Airball
A shot at the basket that misses everything and doesn't touch the rim, backboard or net.

Alley-Oop:
When one player jumps and catches a pass from another player and simultaneously dunks the ball or shoots it in before landing.

And One
When a player gets fouled while shooting and the ball goes in. The player then gets one free throw.

Assist
A statistic that occurs when a player passes the ball to someone who scores after receiving the pass. The passing player earns an assist in the stat sheet.

B

Backboard:
The rectangular piece of wood or fiberglass the rim is attached to.

Backdoor:
An offensive action in which a player without the ball cuts behind a defender and toward the basket.

Bank Shot:
When a player shoots the ball and it bounces off the backboard and into the hoop.

Block (action):
A statistic that occurs when a defensive player stops an offensive player from making a shot by blocking the ball with his or her hand(s).

Block (area of court):
The area just outside of the key in which the rectangular blocks are painted. Also referred to as the post.

Box Out:
When a shot goes up, players use this technique, which involves widening their stance and arms and using their body as a barrier to get in better rebounding position.

Carry
 This penalty, which results in a turnover, occurs when a player holds the ball excessively at the apex while dribbling.

Charge
 This penalty, which results in a turnover, occurs when an offensive player with the ball runs into a stationary defensive player and knocks him or her over.

D

Double Dribble
 This penalty, which results in a turnover, occurs when a player dribbles the ball with both hands. It also occurs when a player dribbles, stops dribbling, and then begins to dribble again.

E

Elbow:
 The area of the court where the free throw line meets the side of the key or paint.

F

Fast Break
An offensive action where a team attempts to advance the ball and score as quickly as possible after a steal, blocked shot or rebound.

Flop:
When a player attempts to draw a foul on an opposing player by acting, fabricating or over-exaggerating the extent of contact.

Free Throw:
A free shot given to a player after a foul or a technical foul. The player shoots from the 15-foot free throw line while the rest of the players line up along the outside of the key.

K

Key: The painted area that makes up the free throw lane. Also referred to as the paint.

L

Lay-Up:
A shot taken close to the hoop, usually when a player is moving toward the basket.

M

Man-to-Man:
A defensive strategy in which each player on the defensive team guards one person on the opposing team.

O

One and One:
When a team has reached the initial foul limit, or the bonus, the next player to get fouled will receive one free throw. If the player makes the free throw, he or she shoots an additional free throw. This occurs in youth, high school and college basketball only.

Outlet:
An offensive strategy in which a player who gathers a defensive rebound passes to a teammate in an attempt to quickly begin the next possession.

P

Paint:
The painted area that makes up the free throw lane. Also referred to as the key.

Post:
The area just outside of the key in which the rectangular blocks are painted. Also referred to as the block.

Press:
A defensive strategy where the defenders guard the opposing team the full length of the court instead of waiting on the opposite side for the offense to come across.

Post Up:
An offensive strategy in which a player gets the ball in the post area with his or her back to the basket.

R

Rebound:
When a player from either team retrieves the ball and gains possession after a missed shot.

S

Screen
An offensive strategy in which a player without the ball stands in the way of a defensive player. The offensive player must remain stationary during the process, or a moving screen will be called and the result will be an offensive foul and a turnover.

Swish
A made basket where the ball avoids the rim and touches nothing but the net, creating a "swish" sound.

T

Three in the Key
A penalty, which results in a turnover, where an offensive player stands inside the key or the paint area for three seconds.

Travel
A penalty, which results in a turnover, where an offensive player moves his or her pivot foot illegally or takes three steps without dribbling the ball.

Turnover
When the offensive team loses possession of the ball by way of an offensive foul, steal or out-of-bounds violation.

Z

Zone Defense

A defensive strategy in which players guard a specific zone or area of the court instead of a specific player on the opposing team.

Hey Little Baller,

Write down a goal you have inside of each basketball. Afterwards, sign your name to show your commitment to reaching your goals.

Signature:_____ Date:_____

Balling With The Smith Brothers!!!

www.ingramcontent.com/pod-product-compliance
Lightning Source LLC
Chambersburg PA
CBHW060757090426
42736CB00002B/58